HAL LEONARD
PIANO METHOD

PIANO FOR TEENS

A Beginner's Guide with Step-by-Step Instruction for Piano

BY JENNIFER LINN

T0039566

To access audio visit:
www.halleonard.com/mylibrary

Enter Code
1646-1308-1463-2958

Orchestrated audio arrangements by Peter Deneff

ISBN 978-1-5400-2305-6

HAL•LEONARD®
7777 W. BLUEMOUND RD. P.O. BOX 13819 MILWAUKEE, WI 53213

Visit Hal Leonard Online at
www.halleonard.com

INTRODUCTION

Welcome to *Piano for Teens*! This book is designed for young adults who want to learn how to play the piano or keyboard faster than ever before. Popular songs like "All of Me," "Hallelujah," "Hello," "Roar," "Shake It Off," "We Will Rock You," and classical favorites like Beethoven's "Für Elise" all include clear instruction allowing students to progress and play each new song with confidence. The clean, simple page layouts ensure that new concepts are clearly presented and easy to follow. Songs progress in a logical sequence so students can learn valuable musical skills while playing music they want to learn.

–Jennifer Linn

ABOUT THE AUDIO

To access the accompanying audio, simply go to **www.halleonard.com/mylibrary** and enter the code found on page 1 of this book. This will grant you instant access to every file. You can download to your computer, tablet, or phone, or stream the audio live—and you can also use our *PLAYBACK+* multi-functional audio player to slow down or speed up the tempo, change keys, or set loop points. This feature is available exclusively from Hal Leonard and is included with the price of this book!

For technical support, please email support@halleonard.com

CONTENTS

PARTS OF THE PIANO

UPRIGHT PIANO

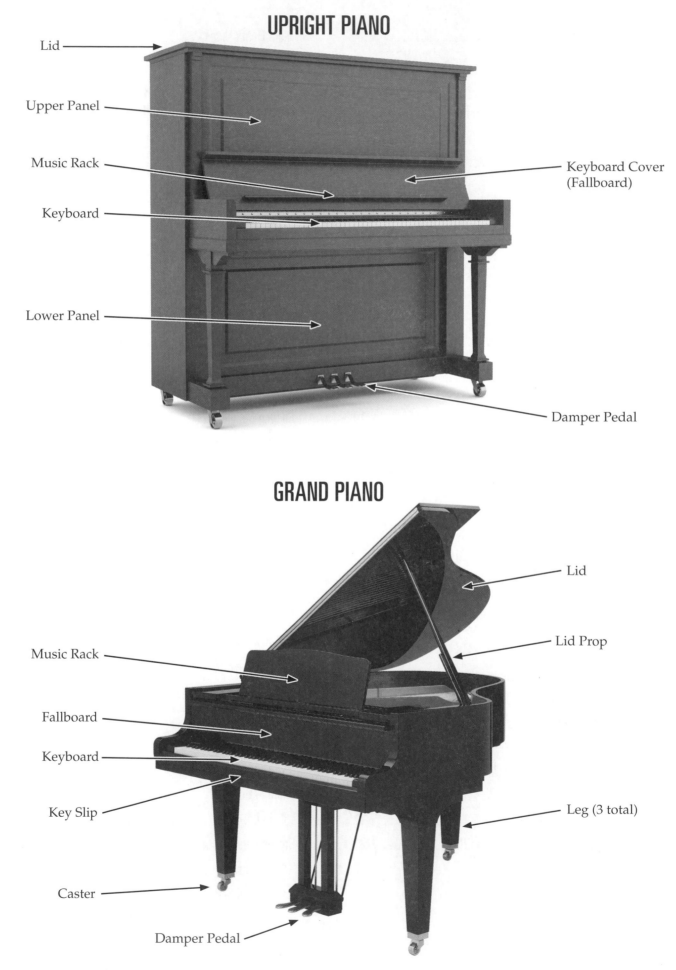

Lid

Upper Panel

Music Rack

Keyboard

Lower Panel

Keyboard Cover
(Fallboard)

Damper Pedal

GRAND PIANO

Music Rack

Fallboard

Keyboard

Key Slip

Caster

Damper Pedal

Lid

Lid Prop

Leg (3 total)

HOW TO SIT AT THE PIANO

- Sit tall on the front half of the bench.
- Lean slightly forward.
- Keep your feet flat on the floor.
- Your knees should be only slightly under the keys.
- Your elbows should be higher than the keyboard level.
- Keep your shoulders relaxed.

GOOD HAND POSITION

- Make sure your wrist and back of the hand form a straight line.
- Curve your fingers so that only your fingertips are touching the keys.
- Use the side tip of your thumb.
- Keep your wrist relaxed and flexible.

FINGER NUMBERS

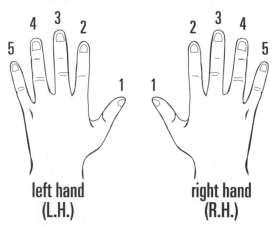

left hand
(L.H.)

right hand
(R.H.)

- Each finger is assigned a number.
- Place your palms together with your fingertips touching.

    Tap 1's (thumbs)

    Tap 2's

    Tap 3's

    Tap 4's

    Tap 5's

- FINGERING: The finger numbers will appear above and below the music notes. These numbers are known as the fingering and are to be followed exactly.

THE KEYBOARD

The keyboard consists of white and black keys. The black keys are arranged in groups of twos and threes.

- Circle all the 2 black-key groups and box all the 3 black-key groups below.
- Play all the 2 black-key groups on your keyboard with your L.H., using fingers 2 and 3.
- Play all the 3 black-key groups with your R.H., using fingers 2, 3, 4.

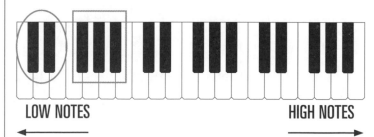

LOW NOTES

HIGH NOTES

RHYTHM IN MUSIC: QUARTER NOTE AND REST

Rhythm in music needs a steady **BEAT**. The quarter note gets one beat of sound and the quarter rest gets one beat of silence.

♩ = 1 beat of sound   𝄽 = 1 beat of silence

Place your R.H. and L.H. 2nd fingers on two white-key D's in the center of your keyboard. Think **"D for doghouse"** to help you remember.

Down stems are for L.H. notes.

Up stems are for R.H. notes.

FEEL THE BEAT

R.H. 2

Feel   the   beat   now!   Keep   it   stead - y.   Keep   it   go - ing   'til   you're   read - y.

2
L.H.

HICCUP RAP

R.H. 2

UH   OH! (hic)   I   think   I   (hic)   just   might (hic) have   the   (hic) hic - cups! (hic)

2
L.H.

6

THE HALF NOTE AND HALF REST

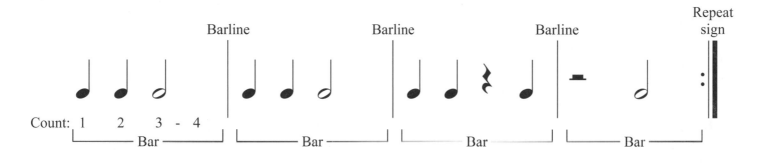

BARLINES divide the music into **BARS**. Tap the rhythm below with your right hand on the closed lid. Remember that the quarter rest is one beat of silence and the half rest is two beats of silence.

WE WILL ROCK YOU

Words and Music by Brian May

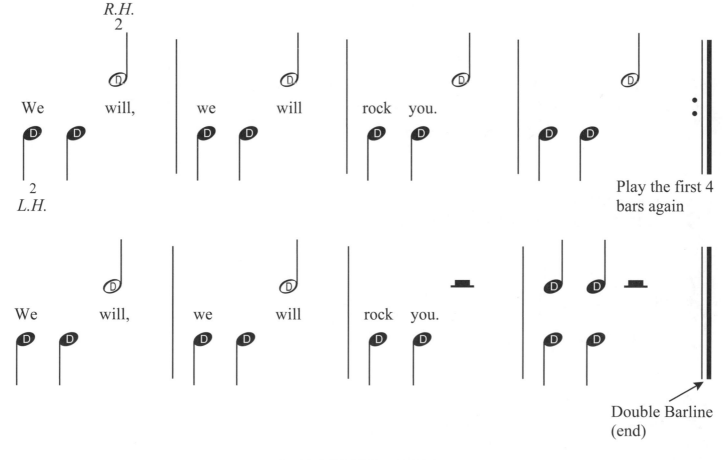

TREBLE STAFF NOTES CDE

- You already know how to find D. The notes C and E are right next door!
- Place your R.H. thumb on middle C and play C D E with fingers 1, 2, 3.
- Now play it backwards (E D C) with fingers 3, 2, 1.
- Play all the C D E's on your keyboard.

TIME SIGNATURE

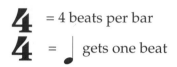

4/4 = 4 beats per bar

4/4 = ♩ gets one beat

The time signature tells how many beats are in a bar, and what kind of note gets one beat.

STAFF

The **staff** is made with 5 lines and 4 spaces.

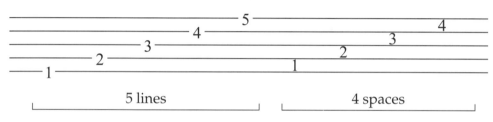

| 5 lines | 4 spaces |

A **line note** has a line in the middle of the note head.

A **space note** fits in between the staff lines.

TOO MUCH HOMEWORK 🔊

Jennifer Linn

BASS STAFF NOTES G AND A

- The 3 black-key group will help you find the G and A.
- With your L.H., "park" fingers 2 and 3 in the "double garage."

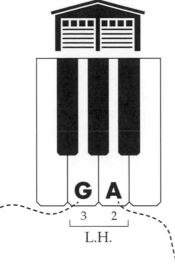

- Remember to play with curved fingers and a rounded hand shape.

GARAGE BAND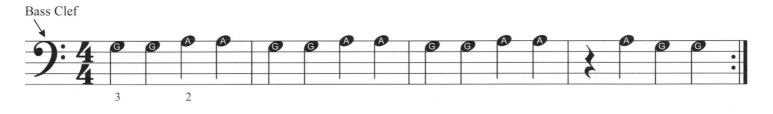

HONKING HORNS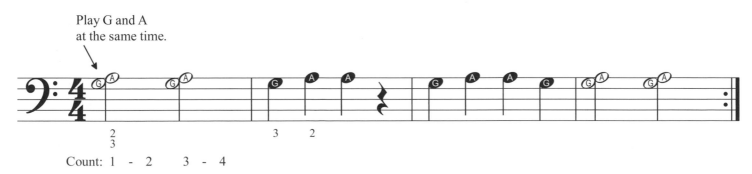

THE GRAND STAFF

The **grand staff** brings the treble staff and bass staff together. The staves are connected by a brace.

brace

WOLFGANG AMADEUS MOZART (1756–1791)

Mozart was a famous classical composer from Austria. By the age of six this remarkable prodigy began composing his own music. He performed through Europe accompanied by his father Leopold and sister Nannerl. He wrote a set of variations based on the French folk song "Ah, vous dirai-je, Maman" popular in his day. Today the tune is better known as "Twinkle, Twinkle, Little Star."

MOZART'S TUNE

Jennifer Linn

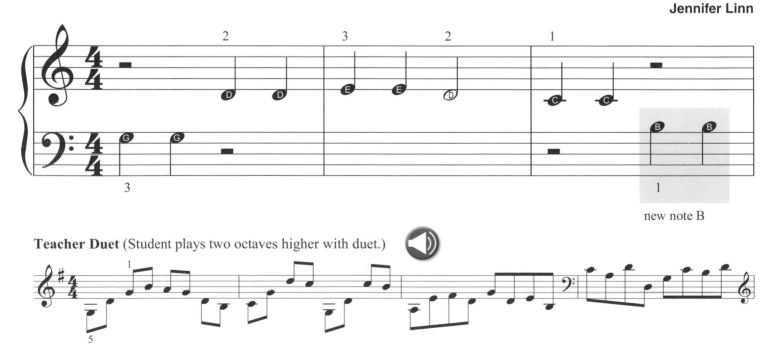

new note B

Teacher Duet (Student plays two octaves higher with duet.)

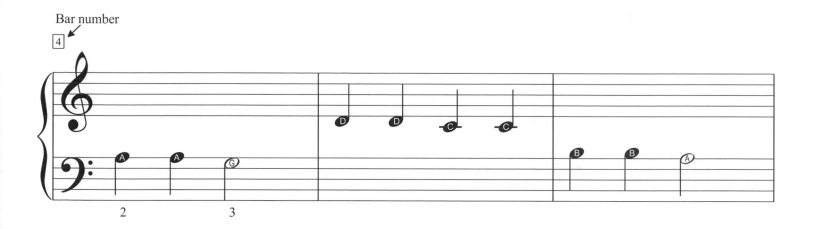

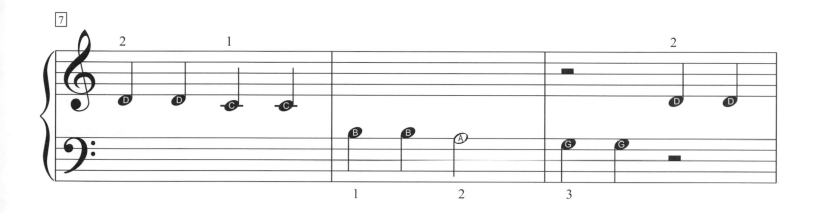

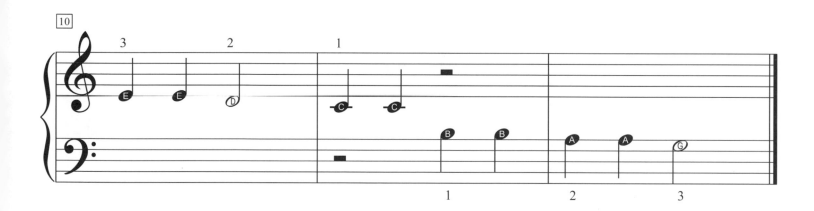

NEW NOTES F AND G

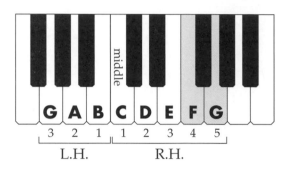

3 2 1 | 1 2 3 4 5

L.H.   R.H.

𝅗𝅥. = 3 beats

DOTTED HALF NOTE

Count: 1 - 2 - 3

TIME SIGNATURE

3/4 = 3 beats per bar

= ♩ gets one beat

IN MY DREAMS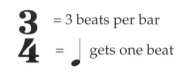

Jennifer Linn

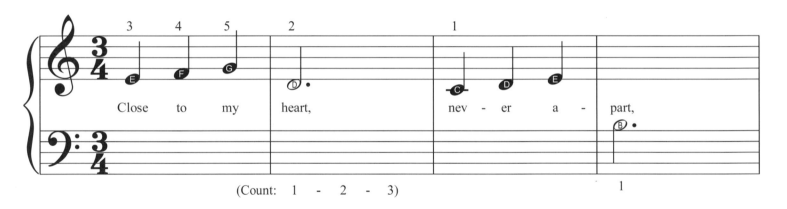

Close to my heart,   nev - er a - part,

(Count: 1 - 2 - 3)

Teacher Duet (Student plays two octaves higher with duet.)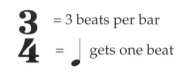

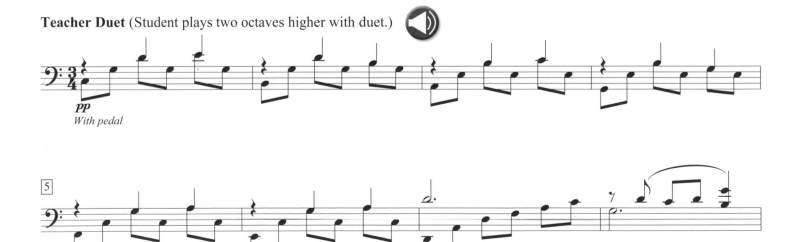

pp
With pedal

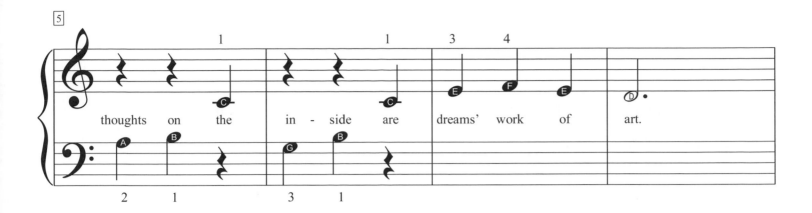

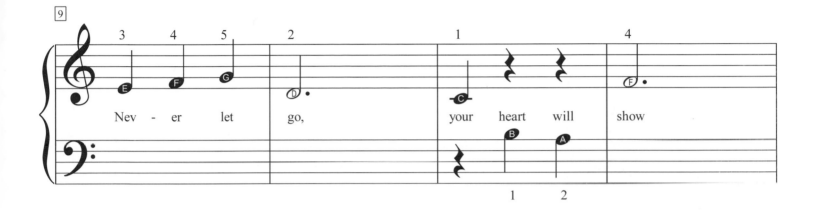

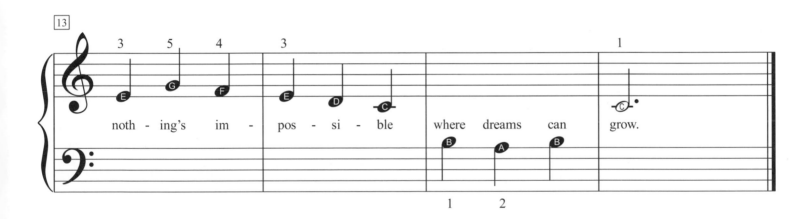

TIES AND SLURS

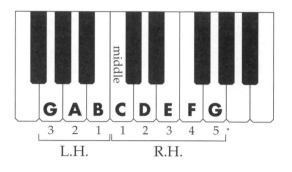

G A B C D E F G
3 2 1   1 2 3 4 5
L.H.   R.H.

TIE

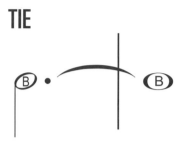

A **tie** joins two note values together. Hold the note for the total number of beats.

SLUR

A **slur** over or under the notes means you play them **legato** (smoothly connected).

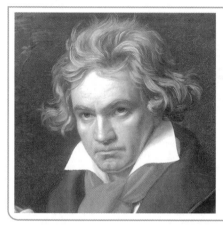

LUDWIG VAN BEETHOVEN (1770–1827)

Beethoven was one of the greatest composers of all time. He wrote almost 400 compositions including this famous melody you will play from his Symphony No. 6 (Pastoral). By the age of 32, Beethoven was aware that he was beginning to lose his hearing but despite his uncertain future, he became more determined to compose his greatest works. Beethoven described the 5th movement from the Pastoral Symphony as "salutary feelings combines with thanks to the Deity."

SYMPHONY WARM-UP

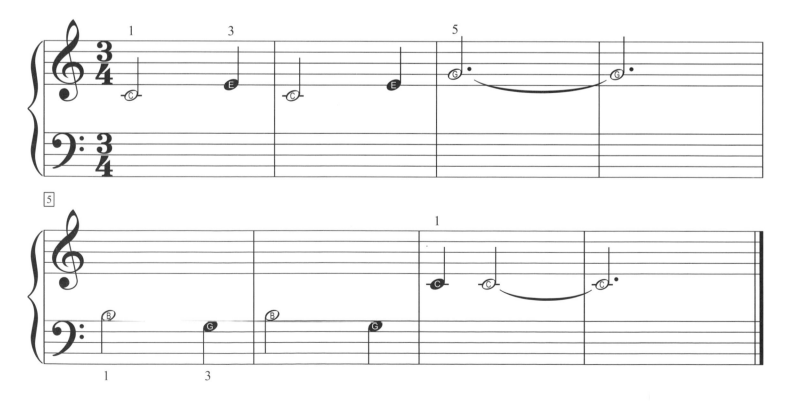

SYMPHONY NO. 6 (Pastoral)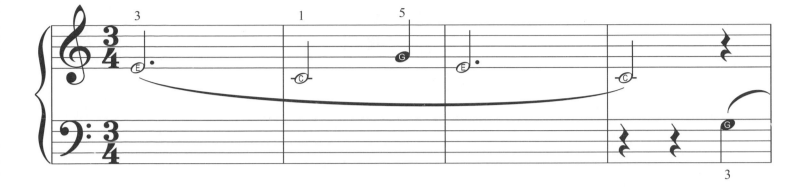
(5th Movement)

Ludwig van Beethoven

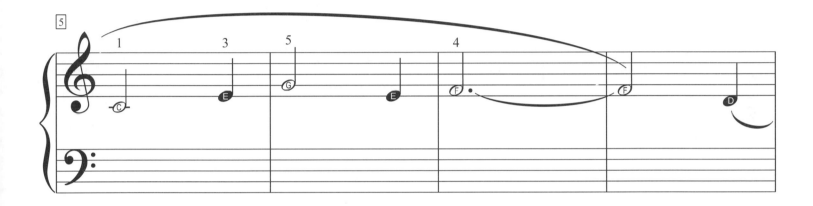

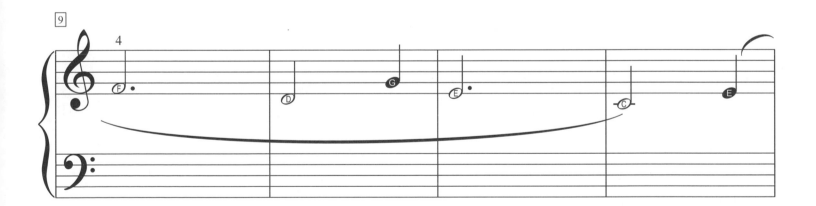

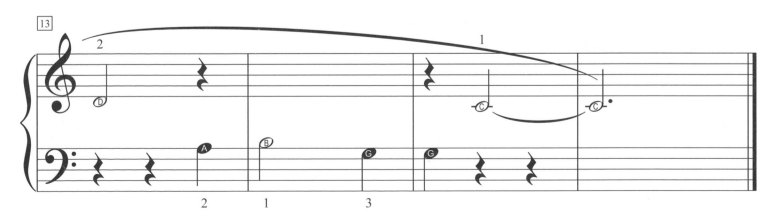

DYNAMICS

Dynamic markings are symbols that tell you how loud or soft to play.

p = Soft (*piano*)

f = Loud (*forte*)

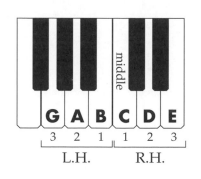

HALLELUJAH WARM-UP

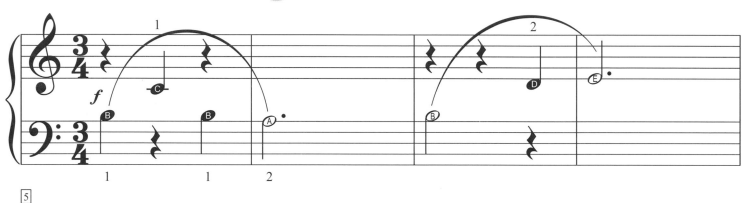

HALLELUJAH

**Words and Music by
Leonard Cohen**

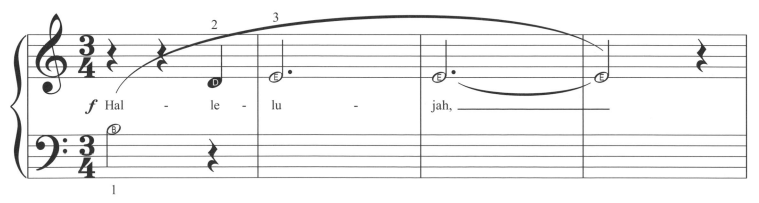

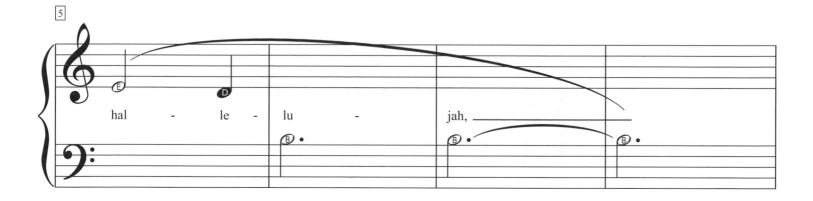

hal - le - lu - jah, _____

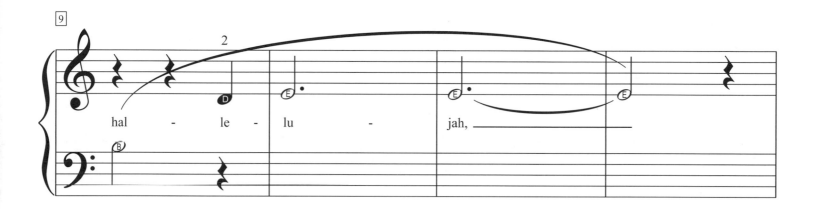

hal - le - lu - jah, _____

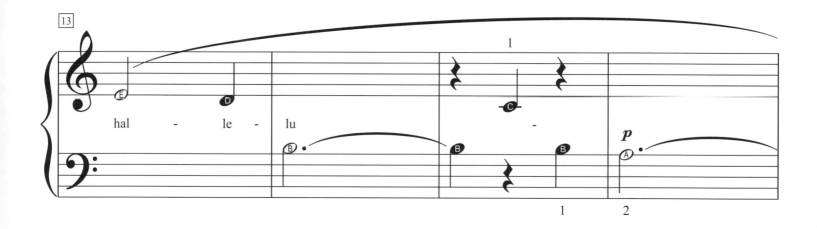

hal - le - lu - _____

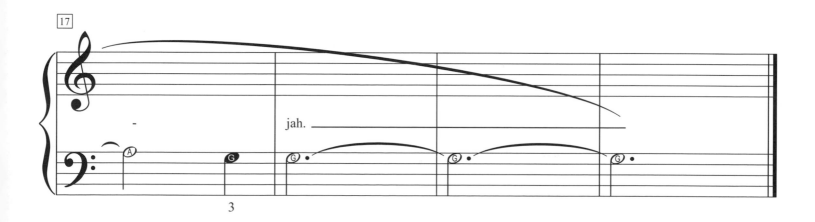

- jah. _____

WHOLE NOTE AND REST

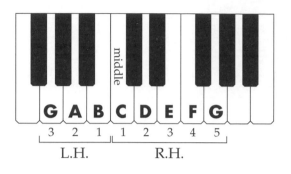

WHOLE NOTE

𝅝 = 4 beats

Count: 1 - 2 - 3 - 4

WHOLE REST

▬ = 4 beats of silence

CAN YOU FEEL THE LOVE TONIGHT
from THE LION KING

Music by Elton John
Lyrics by Tim Rice

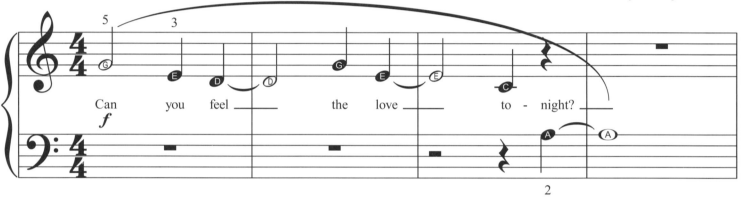

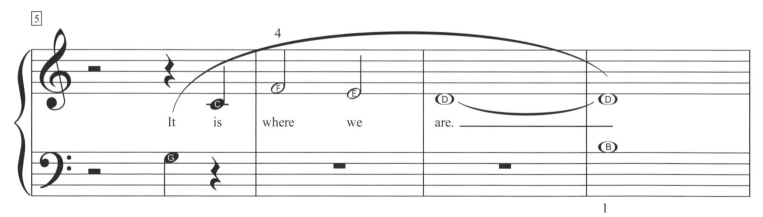

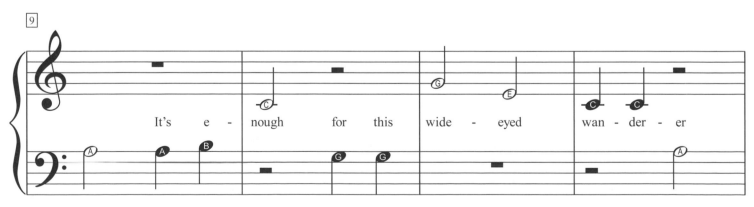

TWO EIGHTH NOTES

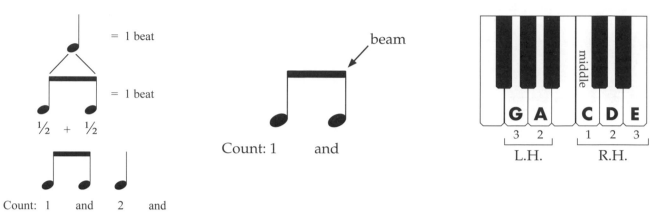

THERE'S A SONG IN MY KEYBOARD 🔊

Jennifer Linn

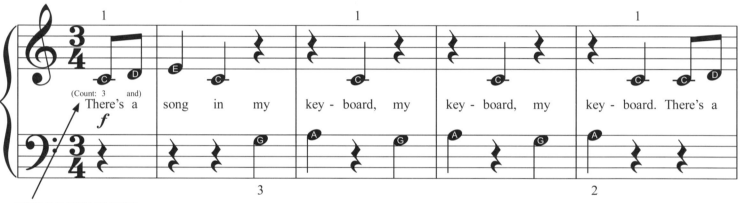

(Count: 3 and)
There's a song in my key - board, my key - board, my key - board. There's a

YOU DO THE MATH!

An **upbeat** is an incomplete bar at the beginning of a song. The missing beats are at the end of the song.

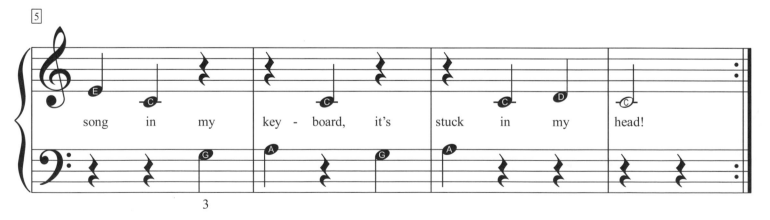

song in my key - board, it's stuck in my head!

ADDITIONAL VERSES

VERSE 2:

Every time that I play it, I play it, I play it.
Every time that I play it, I play it again!

VERSE 3:

Have a headache, a headache, a headache a headache?
Have a headache, a headache, it's time to move on!

FERMATA

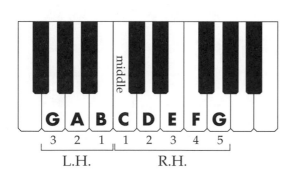

⌢
•

FERMATA

The **fermata** over a note tells you to hold the note a little longer.

HAPPY BIRTHDAY TO YOU

Words and Music by Mildred J. Hill
and Patty S. Hill

A whole rest in
3/4 time is 3 beats

Teacher Duet (Student plays one octave higher.)

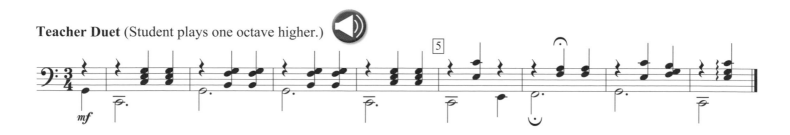

IN REVIEW

Fill in the blanks in the first column with the corresponding symbol letter and definition number.

TERMS

symbol   definition

_____ _____ quarter note

_____ _____ slur

_____ _____ half note

_____ _____ time signature

_____ _____ treble clef

_____ _____ half rest

_____ _____ tie

_____ _____ piano

_____ _____ repeat sign

_____ _____ brace

_____ _____ eighth notes

_____ _____ bass clef

_____ _____ Mozart

_____ _____ double barline

_____ _____ grand staff

_____ _____ whole rest

_____ _____ dotted half note

_____ _____ quarter rest

_____ _____ Beethoven

_____ _____ fermata

_____ _____ forte

_____ _____ upbeat

_____ _____ whole note

SYMBOLS

a.

b. {

c. o

d. 𝄢

e. :‖

f.

g. ⅃

h. 4/4

i. 3/4 ♩ | ♩ | ♩ ♩

j.

k. ♩

l.

m. ♩

n. ▬

o. ⌢

p. 𝄞

q. ▬

r.

s.

t. ‖

u. **f**

v. **p**

w. ♩.

DEFINITIONS

1. two beats of sound

2. composed a set of variations on "A vous dira-jai Maman"

3. one beat of sound

4. play smoothly connected

5. play softly

6. clef for left hand notes

7. tells how many beats are in a bar

8. indicates the end of the piece

9. clef for the right hand

10. two beats of silence

11. four beats of sound

12. hold extra time

13. play it again

14. joins two note values together

15. symbol that joins two staffs together

16. play loudly

17. incomplete bar at the beginning

18. one beat of silence

19. treble and bass staff combined

20. 3 beats of sound

21. two beamed notes equal to one beat

22. wrote the Pastoral Symphony

23. 4 beats of silence

MORE EIGHTH NOTES
MENUET EN ROUNDEAU

Jean-Phillipe Rameau

The L.H. plays in treble clef, but one octave lower than written. Notice that the eighth notes are now beamed in groups of 4. How many beats are in one group of 4 eighth notes?

FOLLOW THE LEADER

Louis Köhler

NOTESPELLING ON THE GRAND STAFF

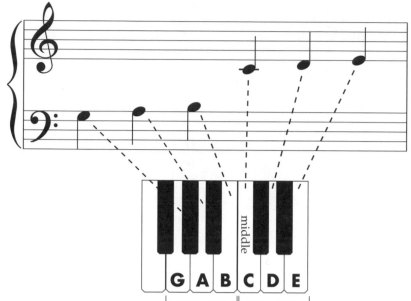

Write the correct note name in the blank below each note.

READING CDE ON THE STAFF

- Now you are ready to play the notes C, D and E while reading from the treble staff.
- Say the note names out loud as you play.

AU CLAIR DE LA LUNE

Sweetly

French Folksong

OH YAY, IT'S FRIDAY

Happy dance

Jennifer Linn

HOT CROSS BUNS

Lively

Traditional

READING GAB ON THE STAFF

- Now you are ready to play the notes G, A and B while reading from the bass staff.

- Say the note names out loud as you play.

IN THE BAG

Jennifer Linn

MERRILY WE ROLL ALONG

Traditional

RHYTHM RAP

Jennifer Linn

Make up your own lyrics to "Rhythm Rap."

MORE NOTESPELLING ON THE GRAND STAFF

Write the correct **note name** in the blank below each note to form words.

_ _ _ _ _ _

_ _ _

_ _ _ _ _ _ _

_ _ _ _ _ _ _

_ _ _ _ _ _

_ _ _

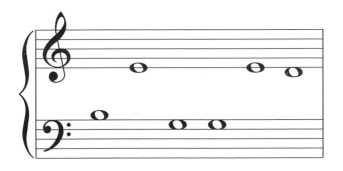

_ _ _ _ _ _

_ _ _ _ _ _

NEW MARKS OF EXPRESSION

pp = Very soft (*pianissimo*)

mp = Medium soft (*mezzo piano*)

mf = Medium loud (*mezzo forte*)

Crescendo means you play gradually louder.

Diminuendo means you play gradually softer.

MOZART ON STAGE

Jennifer Linn

- Find the bar that is missing a whole rest and write in the rest.
- How many half rests are in this piece?

Note to teacher: May be played with the Teacher duet from "Mozart's Tune" on page 10.

SHARING MIDDLE C

NEW L.H. POSITION

Your L.H. thumb will share middle C with your R.H. thumb. Your thumbs will take turns playing the exact same key.

Practice the exercise below. The thumb that is **not** playing should **make room** for the thumb that **is** playing. Do not use both thumbs at the same time.

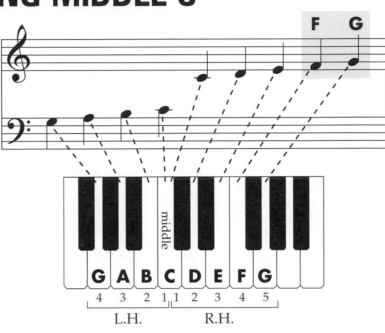

ROCK THAT BOAT

Jennifer Linn

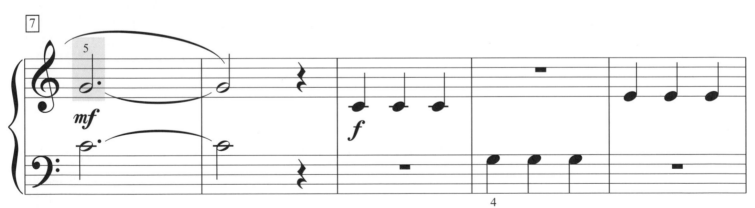

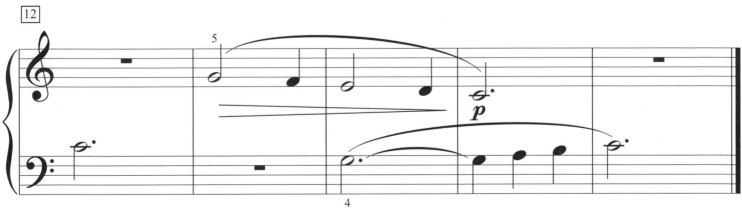

STACCATO

A dot under (or over) a note means to play the note **staccato**. To play **staccato**, release the key immediately, letting your wrist bounce slightly.

staccato dot

REMEMBER

A **slur** over or under the notes means you play them **legato** (smoothly connected).

SHARING MIDDLE C

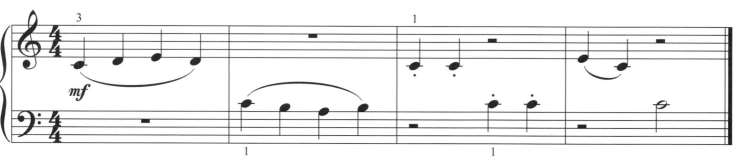

STACCATO WARM-UP

LET IT GO
from FROZEN

Music and Lyrics by
Kristen Anderson-Lopez
and Robert Lopez

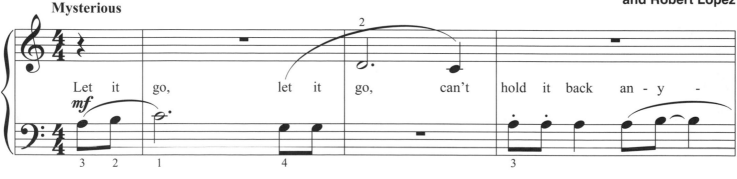

Let it go, let it go, can't hold it back an - y -

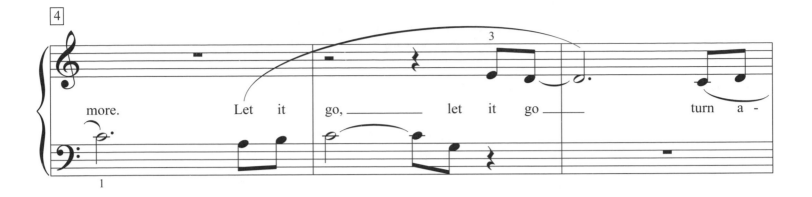

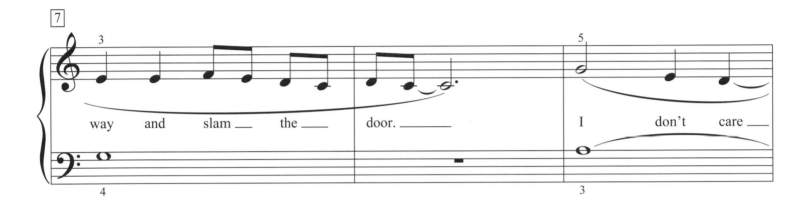

MOVING BEYOND A FIXED HAND POSITION

HAND POSITION SHIFT

In this book, when you see a fingering in a shading triangle, your hand will need to move higher or lower on the keyboard depending on the direction of the triangle.

- There are three new treble clef notes (A, B, C) and one new bass clef note (F) in "All of Me." Fill in the rest of the note names in the shaded boxes.

ALL OF ME

Words and Music by
John Stephens and Toby Gad

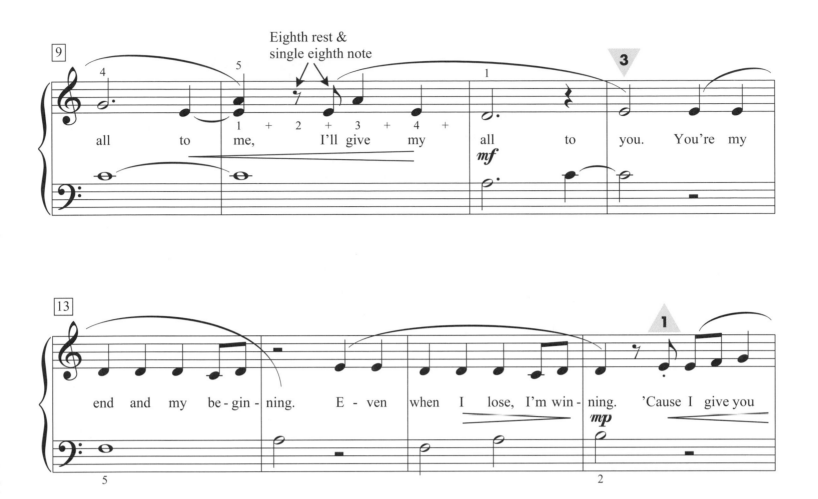

Write the note names.

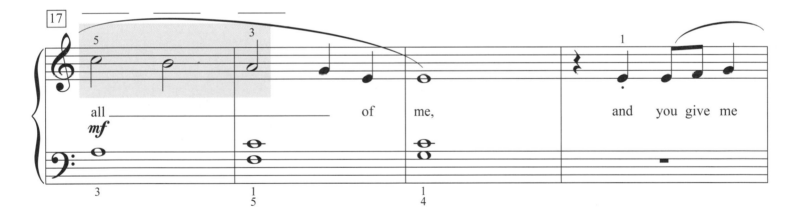

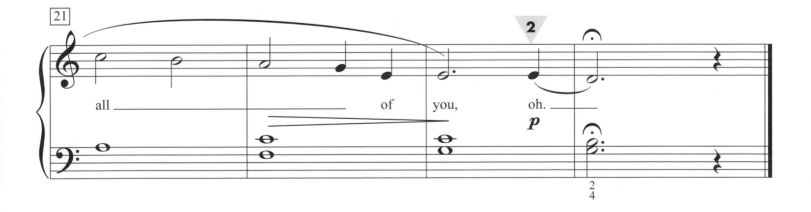

33

SHARPS, FLATS AND NATURALS

SHARP

A **sharp** sign before a note means to play the next key to the right. Once the sharp appears before a note, it remains sharp for the entire bar.

♭ FLAT

A **flat** sign before a note means to play the very next key to the left. Once the flat appears before a note, it remains flat for the entire bar.

♮ NATURAL

A **natural** sign before a note means to cancel the previous sharp or flat.

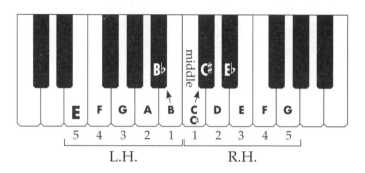

BLACKBIRD

Words and Music by John Lennon and Paul McCartney

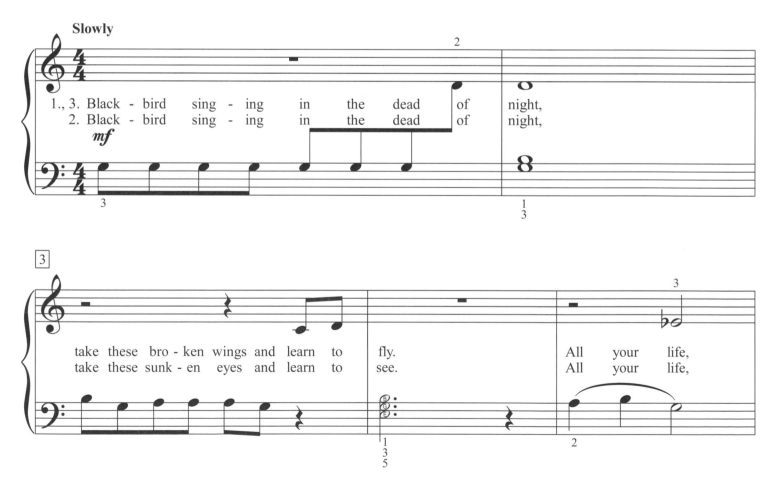

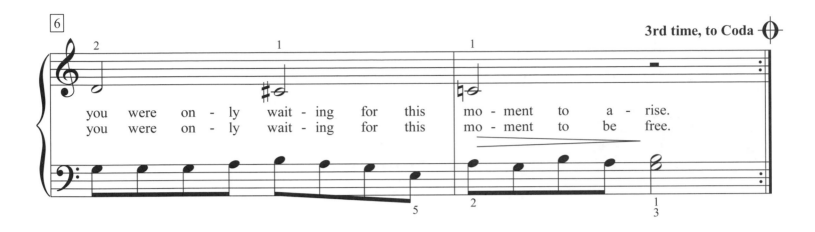

you were on - ly wait - ing for this mo - ment to a - rise.
you were on - ly wait - ing for this mo - ment to be free.

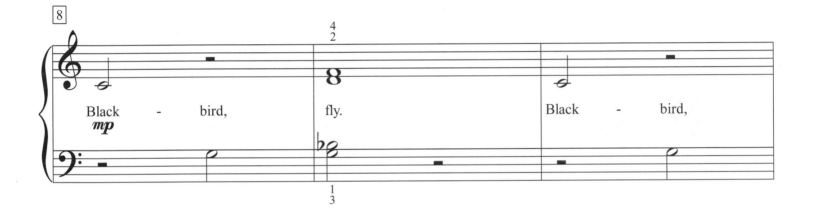

Black - bird, fly. Black - bird,

mp

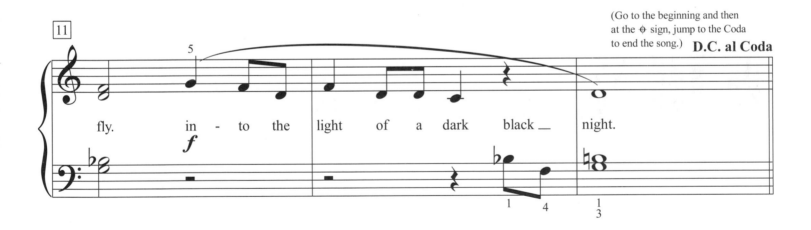

(Go to the beginning and then at the ⊕ sign, jump to the Coda to end the song.) **D.C. al Coda**

fly. in - to the light of a dark black __ night.

f

CODA

you were on - ly wait - ing for this mo - ment to a - rise.

mp

CHORD WARM-UPS

- Practice these L.H. chord warm-ups slowly and use the exact fingering as shown. Keep a rounded hand shape and play with slightly curved fingers. Use your arm weight to synchronize playing 3 keys at once.

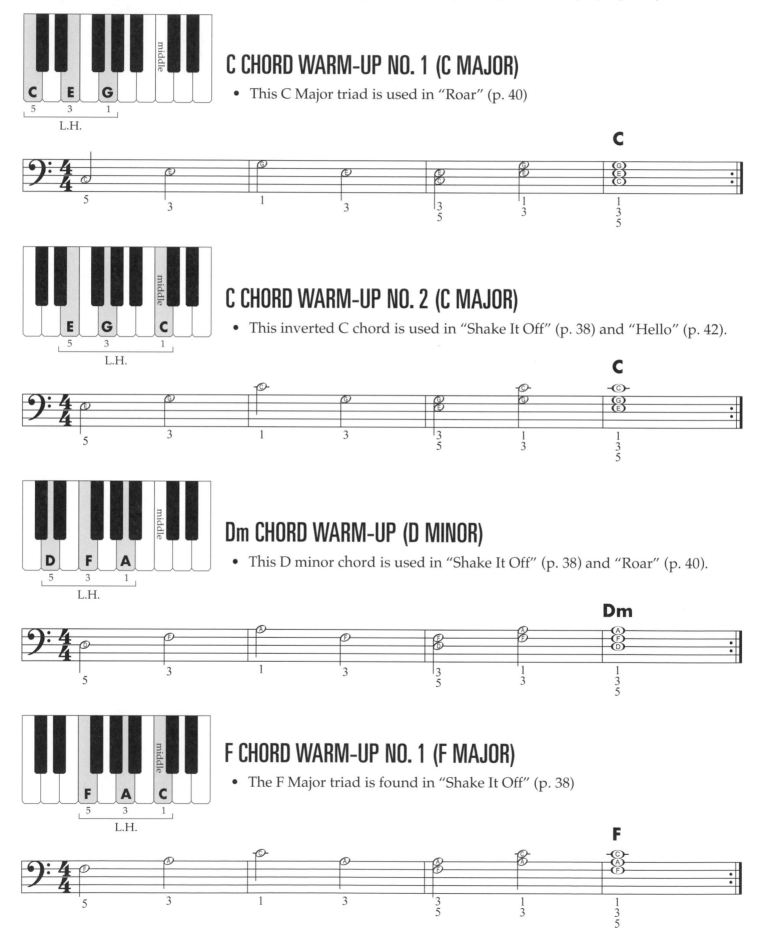

C CHORD WARM-UP NO. 1 (C MAJOR)

- This C Major triad is used in "Roar" (p. 40)

C CHORD WARM-UP NO. 2 (C MAJOR)

- This inverted C chord is used in "Shake It Off" (p. 38) and "Hello" (p. 42).

Dm CHORD WARM-UP (D MINOR)

- This D minor chord is used in "Shake It Off" (p. 38) and "Roar" (p. 40).

F CHORD WARM-UP NO. 1 (F MAJOR)

- The F Major triad is found in "Shake It Off" (p. 38)

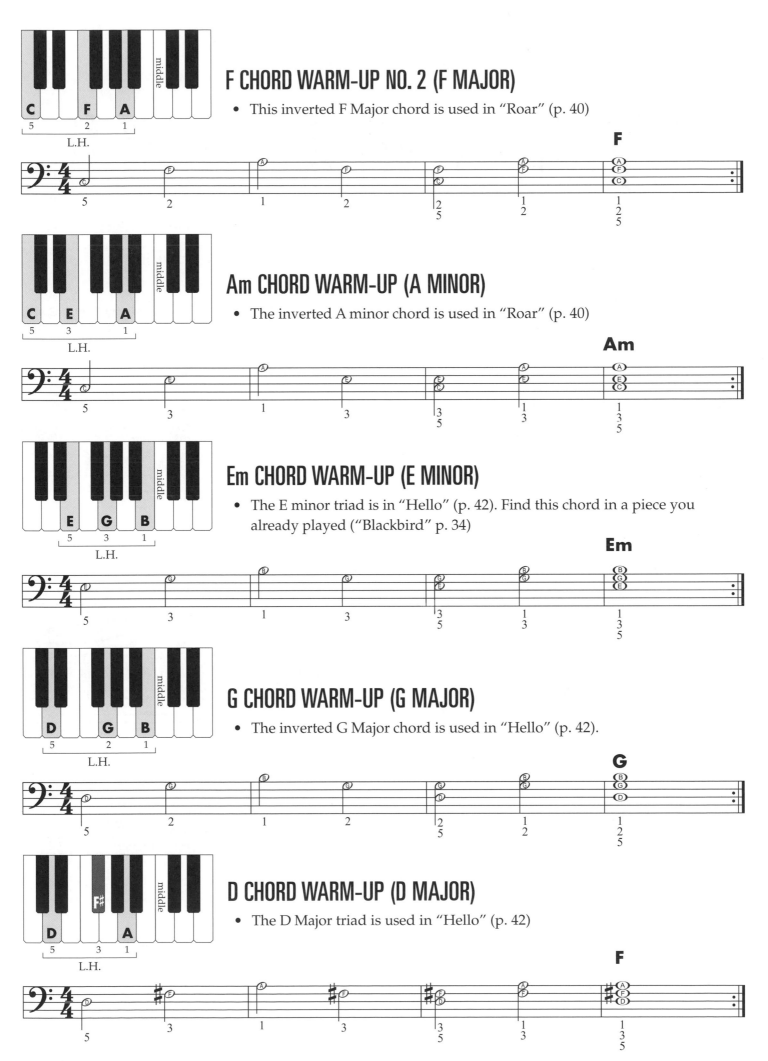

F CHORD WARM-UP NO. 2 (F MAJOR)

- This inverted F Major chord is used in "Roar" (p. 40)

Am CHORD WARM-UP (A MINOR)

- The inverted A minor chord is used in "Roar" (p. 40)

Em CHORD WARM-UP (E MINOR)

- The E minor triad is in "Hello" (p. 42). Find this chord in a piece you already played ("Blackbird" p. 34)

G CHORD WARM-UP (G MAJOR)

- The inverted G Major chord is used in "Hello" (p. 42).

D CHORD WARM-UP (D MAJOR)

- The D Major triad is used in "Hello" (p. 42)

C, F and Dm CHORDS

- Practice the C, F and Dm chords in the chord warm-ups on p. 36 before playing "Shake It Off."

SHAKE IT OFF

**Words and Music by Taylor Swift,
Max Martin and Shellback**

(First time play 1st ending
but skip to 2nd ending on repeat.)

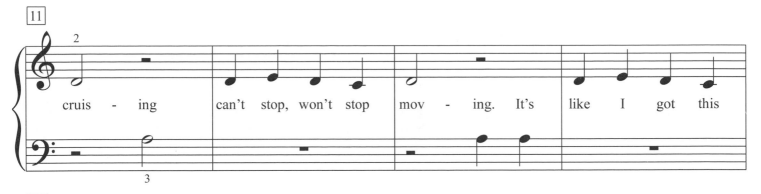

cruis - ing   can't stop, won't stop   mov - ing. It's   like   I   got   this

mu - sic   in   my   mind   say-ing,   "It's gon-na be al - right."   'Cause the

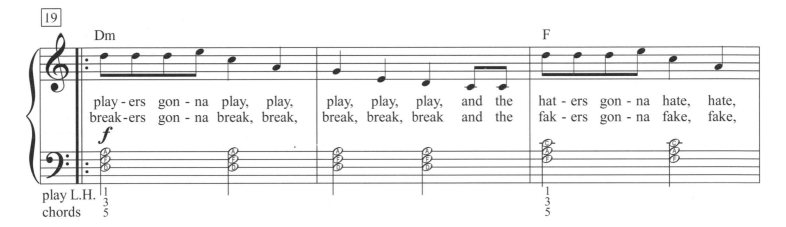

Dm

F

play - ers gon - na play, play,   play, play, play,   and the   hat - ers gon - na hate, hate,
break-ers gon-na break, break,   break, break, break   and the   fak - ers gon - na fake, fake,

play L.H. chords

C

hate, hate, hate,   ba - by   I'm just gon - na shake, shake,   shake, shake,   shake; _   I
fake, fake, fake,   ba - by.   I'm just gon - na shake, shake,   shake, shake,   shake; _   I

1.

2.

shake it off,   I   shake it   off.   Heart -
shake it off,   I   shake it   off.

PUTTING IT ALL TOGETHER

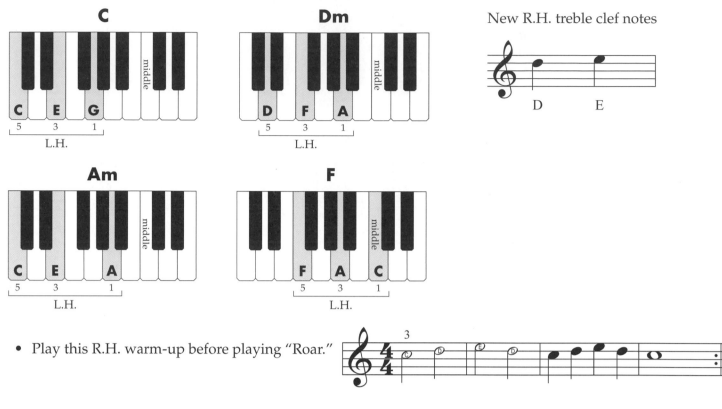

New R.H. treble clef notes

D   E

• Play this R.H. warm-up before playing "Roar."

ROAR

**Words and Music by Katy Perry,
Max Martin, Dr. Luke, Bonnie McKee
and Henry Walter**

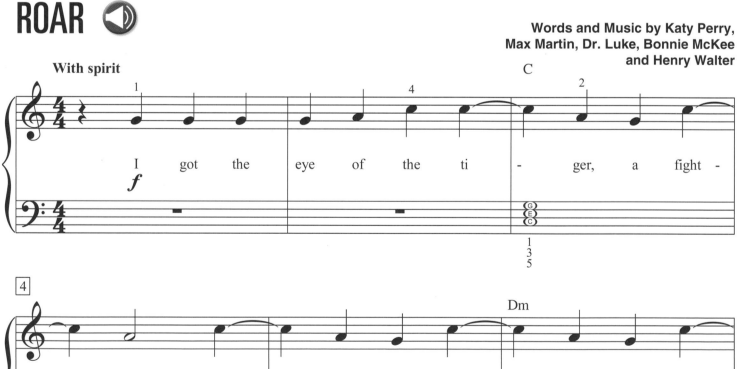

With spirit

C

I got the eye of the ti - ger, a fight -

- er danc - ing through the fire. _____ 'Cause I

Dm

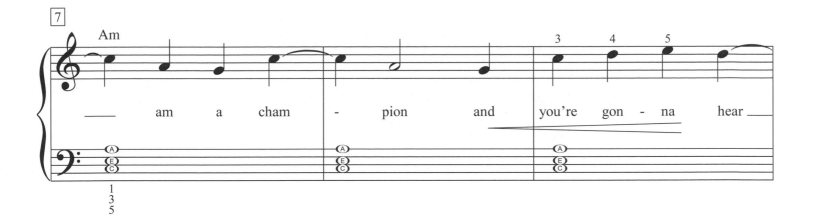

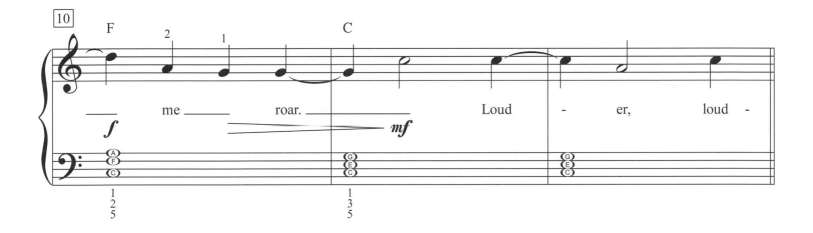

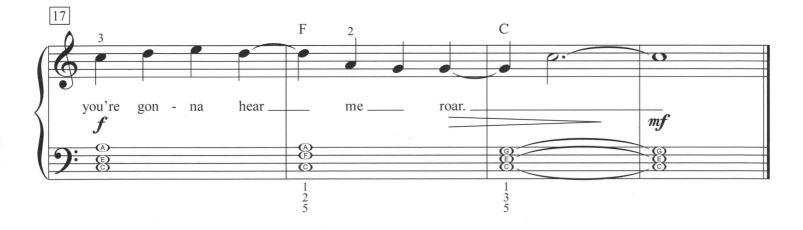

CHORD PATTERNS

The first four chords in "Hello" create a repeating chord pattern throughout the song. Practice these four chords in order until you have the pattern memorized. If you need help, review the chord warm-ups on p. 36-37.

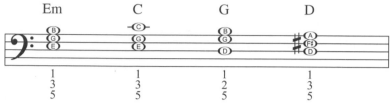

Memorize this chord pattern before playing "Hello."

HELLO

Words and Music by Adele Adkins and Greg Kurstin

BROKEN CHORD PATTERNS

NEW CHORD: E7

DAMPER PEDAL MARKING

When you depress the **damper pedal** (right pedal) it lifts the dampers and allows the piano's strings to ring.

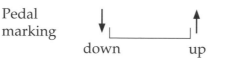

New bass clef notes:

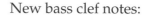

- Practice this warm-up before playing Für Elise.

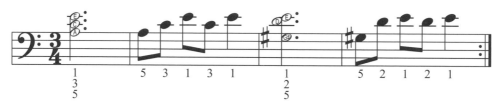

Extra Credit: Name the L.H. broken chords in bars 10-12. _____ _____ _____

FÜR ELISE

Ludwig van Beethoven

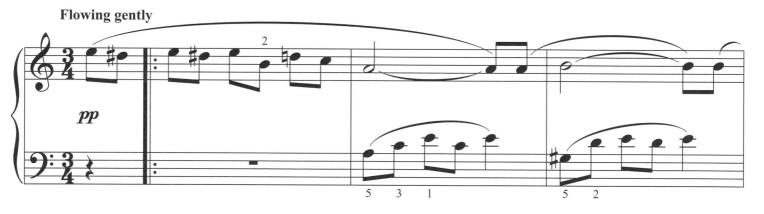

DAMPER AND SOFT PEDALS

CONNECTING PEDAL TECHNIQUE

Keep your right heel on the floor and depress and lift the damper pedal in a singular "up-down" motion as indicated with the notches. This allows for a smooth harmonic change without a break in the sonority.

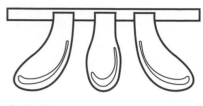

Soft Pedal
(Una Corda)

Damper
Pedal

SOFT PEDAL (UNA CORDA)

The soft pedal (*una corda*) is played with the left foot. Its use is indicated in the music with the abbreviation U.C. and means "one string." You can use this pedal to create a softer or thinner tone color.

OVER THE RAINBOW
from THE WIZARD OF OZ

Music by Harold Arlen
Lyric by E.Y. "Yip" Harburg

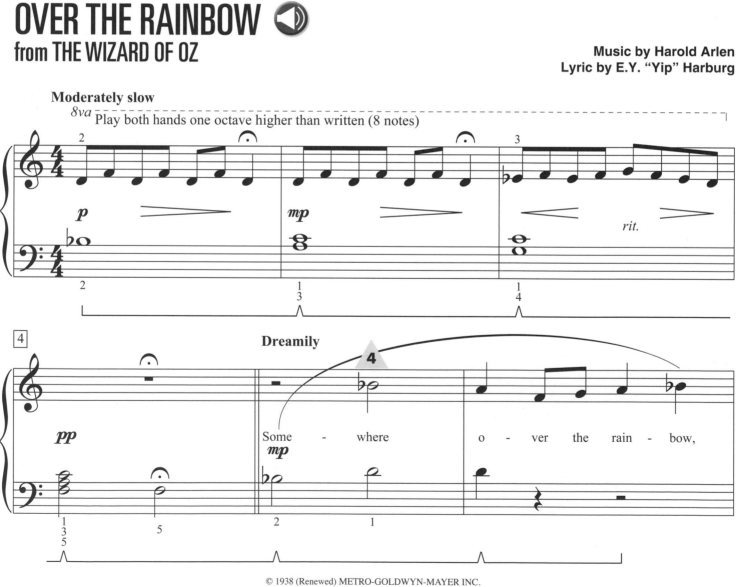